Mind Power
to
Real Estate

Mind Power

to

Real Estate

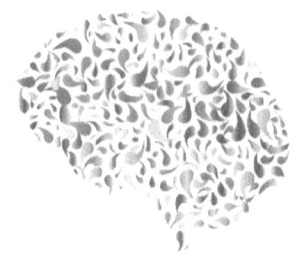

RJ Salerno

Copyright© 2020 by RJ Salerno.

All rights reserved. Printed in the United States of America. No part of this book may be used or reproduced in any manner whatsoever without written permission except in the case of brief quotations embodied in critical articles or reviews.

Limit of Liability/Disclaimer of Warranty: While the publisher and author have used their best efforts in preparing this book, they make no representations or warranties concerning the accuracy or completeness of the contents of this book and specifically disclaim any implied warranties of merchantability or fitness for a particular purpose. No warranty may be created or extended by sales representatives or written sales materials. The advice and strategies contained herein may not be suitable for your situation. You should consult with a professional where appropriate. Neither the publisher nor author shall be liable for any loss of profit or any other commercial damages, including but not limited to special, incidental, consequential, or other damages.

This is a book of nonfiction. No names have been changed, no characters invented, no events fabricated. The methods described in this Book are the author's personal thoughts. They are not intended to be a definitive set of instructions for this project. You may discover that there are other methods and materials to accomplish the same result.

For information, contact RJ Salerno International at:
publishinggenesis@gmail.com

Book and Cover design by RJ Salerno

MIND POWER TO REAL ESTATE

First Edition: August 2020
ISBN: 979-8681953722

10 9 8 7 6 5 4 3 2 1

TABLE OF CONTENTS

Preface 1

Introduction 3

Chapter 1 7

The Power to Succeed First Begins Within the Mind 7

    Begins within the Mind 10

    Renewed in the Mind 13

    Wealth and Happiness have a Design 15

Chapter 2 19

Thought and Imagination 19

    Conscious and Subconscious terms Differentiated 33

    Power of the Subconscious Mind 34

    Reprogramming Your Subconscious Mind 39

        What Is The Subconscious Mind? 40

        How Does this 'Did' Programming Affect You Now? 41

        The Programming Is Still Going On 42

    Impress the Subconscious 46

    Conscious and Subconscious Mind 47

        Thoughts and Ideas to Remember 50

Chapter 3 53

Whatever You Add To, "I Am" 53

    The Power of Words 55

    Disempowering Words 56

- Whatever You Can See, You Can Be 58
- Programming Your Subconscious for Wealth 63

Chapter 4 67

New Career Statistics 67

- Sales Technique 69
- Money and Resources 72

Chapter 5 77

Naysayers and No 77

- Positivity Yourself 78
- Win with Rejection 80
- Great Success Affirmations 82

About the Author 85

PREFACE

This book is dedicated to the aspiring Real Estate Agent, the one who is in his or her heart, searching for a pathway to success. I have a long list of people in my life to give thanks to *(who believed in me)* as the inspiration and source for this book *Mind Power to Real Estate*.

I have seen miracles happen to men and women from all walks of life all over the world. Miracles will happen to you, too - when you begin using the magic power of your subconscious mind. This book is designed to teach you that your habitual thinking and imagery mold, fashion, and create your destiny.

Today you can change everything in your career if you dare to believe in the extraordinary and imagination of what is possible. Remember, words have POWER!

I could only hope that books like this one and also the *Art of the Open House*™ will have a lasting impact on you as it did for me. As I write about the ideas and thoughts of the power of the mind in this book, I wish the revelations of knowledge could have been experienced much sooner in my own life.

It gives me great pleasure to share my experiences of success and failure through my travels in real estate. My hope for you with what I share will either influence your real estate career positively and/or ultimately transform the thinking of life with the power of your mind.

The power of the mind not only has the ability to influence someone's career in real estate, but frankly, it transcends and affects everything we know within our reality and world for good. All creation of thought begins within the mind! Good, bad, or indifferent a thought will manifest through this five senses world as the end result. If you are new to real estate, how much do you believe positive thought will play into your new career?

A person's destiny cannot be seen if the mind is stuck in the past, learn from the past, live in the present, and create a new future. To the future achievements and success may the road in front of you, now have clarity.

If there any great takeaway from this book, it would be, "If you think you are a success, a success you will be."

INTRODUCTION

Fear is the #1 largest obstacle in someone's career, and the feeling of fear has the power to prevent someone from realizing his or her true untapped potential. Where does this fear come from? All fear-based thinking begins within one's mind stemming from one's negative inner thoughts. Where do the source for all these inner negative inner thoughts come from? An outside source! For example, other people and what their perceptions maybe of themselves and their beliefs or opinions involving you. They can be the very source of the fear-based thinking and contention inside of you. One must learn to free themselves from the obstacles of any negative thinking before one can visualize the road to success.

Ask yourself, what would it feel like if you were the real estate agent, you wanted to be? Can you visualize seeing your name listed at the top in the production of your real estate company, as the real estate broker congratulates you for your efforts? What is the sensation inside of you as the commission check is placed into your hands? Do you even believe it's possible? And the answer is

YES! If you believe that, "I AM" successful, then you MUST be. If you believe that "I AM" a real estate superstar home listing machine, then you MUST be. If you think you are, you WILL be. That is the Mental Law of the Mind, and it must come to past into your reality!

Things to Remember

- Every thought is a cause, and every condition is an effect.
- A person must practice separating oneself from the negative moods and thoughts during all the troubles and disasters of daily life.
- If you can imagine it and you visualize it, you can create it.
- Change your thoughts, and you change your destiny.
- Arm yourself with the knowledge and understanding of the mind, and all other things will happen for one's good.

You are the sum total of your own thoughts. Only you can keep from entertaining negative thoughts and imagery in the mind. The way to get rid of darkness is with light; the way to overcome cold is with heat; the way to overcome a negative thought is to substitute for a good thought. Affirm the good and the bad will disappear.

As we move forward together in this book, my hope is that you, as the reader may find not only the solutions herein being sought but also find the true power allusively hidden in one's mind. Best wishes to your career endeavors!

Your very word can bless your real estate business.

Chapter 1

The Power to Succeed First Begins Within the Mind

When deciding to launch a new career in the real estate industry, it is essential first to analyze the very reasons for choosing this career. The answer to the question of, "Why choose real estate?", becomes the driving force to whether success or failure will be achieved of this new exciting career. There may be dozens of reasons for selecting a career in real estate.

Have you thought about your potential driving force?

For many, the possibilities can be a very lucrative and rewarding business model. As the agent continues to build his or her business, residual income becomes a factor while growing a referral base, which has the ability to support a well trained real estate agent for the many years to come.

Nothing can be any more gratifying and rewarding than to put in full display all your expertise, skill, plus knowledge when helping someone achieve buying or selling a home; to help them accomplish their desired DONE.

How would it feel if you were the real estate agent you wanted to be right now? Can you imagine in your mind as you see your name listed among the top producers of your office? Try to imagine the feeling of your real estate broker congratulating you as you visualize him or her shaking your hand as they hand that well-deserved award to you for a job well done. How would that feel inside? Probably sensational!

Interview any well accomplished real estate agent in the business, and he or she will undoubtedly agree while beaming with a smile acknowledging all their successful accomplishments done.

Doubtful, there is anyone that arrives into real estate who does not feel they too cannot realize their definition of accomplishment and reward. For many who select this career path will typically assume that there is some external solution to excel. Some may believe there is some type of preparation that will instantly spring them to the top of production within their real estate office. And, yes, there are plenty of GREAT training courses, books, and gurus available in developing your real estate skills and knowledge. When I began my career in mid-2002 to say I attempted everything, that would be an understatement. Understand, everything you will ever need *(belief, faith, and imagination)* is within you, inside from the very beginning.

Whether it is working with property listings or focusing on the perspective of buyers, no matter what real estate material or techniques are studied, if one pursues without including the Mind Science to it, I can assure you, a promising career in real estate is over before it had the chance to begin.

Don't believe it?

All one needs to do is survey just 3 or 4 agents from a sea of thousands to find out why they didn't make it. More times than not to those former real estate agents, many will usually explain the material taught, the real estate coaches and company training were fantastic!

So, what happened?

It all began within the mind. They had believed they would make it but did not VISUALIZE it. They had faith they would succeed but did not FEEL it inside! The reason for this lack of faith on the part of a person is that he or she looks at the desired situation through the consciousness of his or her present limitations. Therefore, he or she naturally sees it as an impossible accomplishment. One must have faith in self.

While we are on the subject of when success first begins with the mind, be cautious of the naysayers. These types of people will say you cannot do anything right in their eyes. I will spend more time later with these naysayers.

Begins within the Mind

The purpose of one understanding the mind science of all things is to bring about a renewal in thinking or mental change in that individual. Such a change cannot take place until the individual first discovers the self-inside that he or she would want to change. This discovery can be made only through an uncritical observation of his or her reactions to life. The total of these reactions defines the individual's state of consciousness, and it is the individual's state of consciousness that attracts the situations and circumstances of his or her life.

Power of the mind is best summarized in Dale Carnegie's book: How to Win Friends & Influence People – "Everyone in the world is seeking happiness – and there is one sure way to find it. That is by controlling your thoughts. Happiness does not depend on outward conditions. It depends on inner conditions."

A person must practice separating oneself from the negative moods and thoughts during all the troubles and disasters of daily life. No one can be different from what he or she is now unless one begins to separate oneself from his or her present reactions and to identify oneself with his or her desire. Detachment from negative states of thinking and assumption of the wish fulfilled must be practiced in all the blessings and cursing of life.

Faith is defined, "the ascent of the mind or understanding to the truth." Faith doesn't question—faith knows.

"Faith is the substance of things hoped for, the evidence of things not seen." The full meaning of that statement must be understood. If the meaning were understood, a person would have no problem in accomplishing his or her desire. However, faith is the actual substance of that which is hoped for. It is the evidence of the thing you want, which you do not see in the outer world. That which you want to do or be has already been created. Therefore, it actually does exist. It is possible to bring into your world anything with imagination by your belief that you already have it. Faith that what you want is already a fact is the means by which you activate the invisible state. All things of reality are possible through the use of positive thought and imagination.

In the many years of real estate and the sales profession in general, I have heard a multitude of reasons ranging from, it's too hard, to the leads are crummy, I never get any breaks, that person gets all the luck and on and on! Usually, the excuses said by the person in this state will likely blame someone or something other than him or herself as the root cause. It is called an external excuse and they are about as useful as a game of hand grenades and horses.

Some people may say that luck has something to do with it. I'm sure you've heard people say, "He was at the right place at the right time" or "She was just lucky."

Actually, there is no such thing as luck. Luck is just the receiving of goodness in your life that you don't have an explanation for. The truth is that everything that you have in your life is because of your subconscious mind. The subconscious is the single most powerful part of the human mind.

Your subconscious also plays an important part in your financial life. Have you ever come across people who always had money, no matter what?

Some may have been frugal people, but I'm sure you've seen those who were rich, yet were also big spenders. And then you've seen those who always worked hard but were still broke. Then there are people who hardly ever work and always have money.

What's going on here?

The truth is it has to do with their subconscious…their inner financial thermostat is set on a certain level others seem to miss.

Renewed in the Mind

However, to receive the maximum benefit from all the available training in real estate, one must be renewed in one's mind first. A person must free himself or herself from the lack and limitation of beliefs and ideas, disregard all negative thoughts, and cast aside all doubt. The game of Real Estate is a mental world, and one must have ALL their faculties of the mind performing at 100%. One must start with an idea using imagination to give form and definition of that idea focusing on visualization techniques that bring the idea into a desired attainable goal.

Spend some time genuinely analyzing the TOP 3 reasons for entering this new career and list the TOP 3 goals you would like to achieve within the 1st year. Doing this will help kindle the imagination and visualization processes within your mind to help manifest a pathway to realizing the success desired. When someone says they have a burning desire to succeed, in most cases, they don't understand what the mechanics behind this "burning desire" to achieve are. When all is analyzed, most likely, the #1 reason someone has been attracted to a career in real estate is the thought of success.

For one to excel in this industry, they must visualize enjoying the good that one desires, and impress upon the subconscious mind all that is desired, making yourself FEEL that you are who deserves the good that's desired to be, to do and to have. Some may call it daydreaming or an active imagination, and I will say many of the things we currently own or have in our possession were, but once someone's imagination is brought forth into the physical world, we all know.

Wealth and Happiness have a Design

Just as a building has a blueprint, so does a wealthy, happy, and fulfilling life. Envision that you have bought a new house and home for your loving family, and you have even acquired a world-renowned interior designer to help spruce the place up, so to speak.

You love what your interior designer has come up with and decide to follow his instructions exactly as outlined by his blueprints. You oversee the entire renovation procedure, up to the point that you check each and every material that's bought to ensure that they are topnotch through and through so that your renovated home will last you a long, long time.

With that said and done, isn't it only reasonable or commonsensical to pay the same level of meticulousness to your thought generation and prayers; following your life's blueprint to the letter to make sure you will live wealthy and happy for the rest of your life?

Your subconscious records every experience as a memory of sorts, so your past experiences tend to serve as your mental framework or the foundation of who you are and what type of mindset you have. If your mindset is filled with trauma, poverty, anxiety, troubles, and fears or you yourself are a pessimistic individual, you will quickly discover that you are building a mental framework that is destined for either failure or mediocrity, because your past worries and stress remain as blockades that limit your potential as a human being. This is especially true if you have restrictive beliefs and negatively reinforced convictions.

What you slip into your subconscious mind, through your conscious thoughts, determines how many positive outcomes and maximum payoffs you will get in your life. In fact, that is the most straightforward and easy way to have a happier life.

An optimist is a person who realizes his full potential as a human being by providing his subconscious with his "Never give up" attitude and a motivated mind that's always searching for opportunities for improvement instead of resigning itself to a limited and constrained "reality".

Your conscious thoughts are not audible or visible, but these are the blueprints your subconscious mind follows, regardless of how constructive or detrimental they are to your person.

Luckily, the activation and reprogramming of your subconscious mind happens all the time. In fact, your conscious mind determines your mindset and mental framework, thanks to what is contained inside it. Every minute of every day is an opportunity for you to add positive thoughts and motivational concepts to your head, so that it could go straight to your subconscious mind, which will then help you make your aspirations become a reality.

Revise your blueprint by changing your perspective and mindset if things are not going your way. In order to bring success back in your life, you should have the proper mindset for it. Do not underestimate the power of positive thinking, because every action or dream starts from a mere thought or concept, and having negative thoughts merely destroys your motivation to improve your lot in life.

The thoughts you think, that you will become.

Chapter 2

Thought and Imagination

The intensity that is invested in the visualization technique and feeling of the wish fulfilled combined determines if success or failure that one will be achieved. One cannot just have the visualization without defining feeling to the technique or vice versa and command victory. Think of it in this way. Join the thought "visualization", and feeling "desire" together, and you have the wish fulfilled.

Try to reminisce somewhere in the distant past of when you might have a longing, a strong want, or a desire to see fulfilled. Can you feel inside the definition felt and thought that went into it as the visualization was pressed upon your mind? Do you remember that feeling, the anticipation of waiting, knowing it was going to happen? What happened?

Most likely, it came to past, and what was being desired became fulfilled! Remember, marry the thought "visualization" and feeling "desire" together, and you have the wish fulfilled.

- Eliminate fear, doubts, and negative thinking from your consciousness and welcome love, joy, and wellbeing of thought!
- Daily take part in positive affirmations ' that reach down past your conscious mind and into your subconscious mind where they can do the most good!
- Use techniques that actually trick your subconscious mind into paying attention – and getting the message.
- Become definite about what you want from your real estate career --- and YOU WILL KNOW HOW TO GET IT – by using your power of visualization!

If it is home listings you're desiring and searching for, you don't need to know a thing or even know how it is to happen. One only needs to use the imagination of possibilities and visualize in your mind's eye the events and steps that need to unravel to make that home listing happen. Put the definition of strong belief and feeling into that desire in seeing you acquire that home listing repeatedly in your subconscious, even if the five senses around you denies the facts, with enough time IT WILL COME TO PASS! Your visualization, your belief, will go before you and lead you to all the ways and means of manifesting the desires of your heart.

If you want to add more home listings to your production, then you need to visualize more frequency and expand the feeling of seeing in your mind that it is DONE! It all first begins within the mind.

> *"Imagination is more important than knowledge."*
>
> ~Albert Einstein

> *"Imagination is the very gateway to reality."*
> ~William Blake

Everything you see in the five senses world we all live in has been brought to this world by someone's imagination. EVERYTHING! Therefore, the Power of Thought has everything to do with our lives and, importantly, your new career in real estate. Approach your career, knowing that all things are possible to you because you are all imagination, and imagination creates reality. Knowing what you want, imagine you have it. Knowing what you want to be, imagine you are it. Subjectively appropriate your objective hope, and you have assumed the reality you did not have.

Admittedly, the excitement of a new career, coupled with the multitude of hours into learning and studying to pass the state real estate licensing exam, can give one the illusion to the beginnings of success. It was for me! But I assure you, for many, this is where the calm before the storm begins. I don't say this lightly to intimidate or scare someone from this career path, but the fact is that less than 20% succeed in the 1st year of real estate.

Many real estate gurus will focus on the design and technique of their various programs, and yes, the training may be superior. Still, without studying the Mind Science behind what moves a person, all the training in this world is useless. This is a typical shortlist of the duties and methods taught to the new agent coming into real estate. Usually, the agent will be trained in the details of how to write sales contracts and listing agreements and prepare for listing appointments and planning for open houses. Techniques on how to prospect for home buyers and sellers, search for FSBO's and expired home listings, mail out postcards to prospects and nearby neighbors. There are many great training methods and real estate coaches in expediting this knowledge of real estate; I feel more could be done; maybe by adding the Mind Science behind it, possibly everyone could benefit.

In my journeys, I had plenty of naysayers tell me I wouldn't succeed in real estate. I even had a close relative of mine tell me I was a fool and gave me a compelling story as to why a career in real estate was ludicrous. Nonetheless, one must press on in this game called life, but first arm yourself with the knowledge and understanding of Mind Power, and all other things will automatically happen for one's good.

> *"Proper visualization by the exercise of concentration and willpower enables us to materialize thoughts, not only as dreams or visions in the mental realm but also as experiences in the material realm."*
>
> ~ Paramahansa Yogananda

> *"If you can imagine it and you visualize it, you can create it."*
>
> ~ Anonymous

By the technique of "visualization," a person can direct the attention of the mind toward the good being desired. In doing so, use the creativity of imagination to captivate the full experience. Develop the technique of visualization. Learn to use the imagination to "see" yourself already being, doing, and having the good, which you desire.

If looking for excuses for failure, you will always find them, for you find what you seek. It is effortless to throw in the towel. A real estate agent may face many "NO's" before coming upon that one "YES" to justify all the hard work for that YES. Make no mistake; you may believe it was all your persistence and activities that accomplished that "YES," but it wasn't. It all first began within the mind with your imagination. You pictured that whole thing FIRST in your mind's eye of imagination with the finality being the "YES" because you visualized it and felt it so. That is where the real power lays, but it is easily overlooked.

There are so many different types of people with varying backgrounds from a retail store clerk to a homemaker to Lawyer and everything else in-between, who enter into real estate every day as a profession. Success in this field of real estate has nothing to do with education, family up bring, or social status. I have seen people who have barely graduated high school excel in real estate where others with a Master's Degree from a prestigious college do not excel. Why is that? It's not to say having the degree or nothing at all makes the difference, but if we are going to have a hard look at what makes someone successful, we must focus more in-depth. We must focus on the mind and what its inner conversation is genuinely trying to say to us!

All of us have an inner conversation that plays in our mind every day. Backed by science, it is said that the human brain in 1 day may experience between 65,000 to 80,000 thoughts. With the mind experiencing 65,000 plus thoughts, rest assured there will be plenty of inner conversation too. This could be a positive conversation or a negative conversation. You know what I mean. You may be walking on a sidewalk, and you pass someone as they too are walking by, and maybe you don't like their appearance, perhaps they have a funny shirt on or a hat you don't like, AND right there it just happened — your inner conversation playing out right in your mind as the person passes you. You can almost hear ALL those thoughts, and as automated, your inner conversation can be we don't pay much attention to it.

If one could only control these inner conversations morning, noon and night. Stop for one moment and ask yourself, what am I thinking now? Our inner conversation within our minds can make us or break us, and we don't even realize it. So if inwardly someone might be saying, I can be successful, I don't know how, but in my mind, I'm already a success. What has this person done? They have denied their five senses of this world and beginning with their imagination declaring the presence of SUCCESS for their life! All reason and logic may deny the facts of a person's current state of consciousness, but one believes with all faith it will harden into fact in this physical world as reality.

Don't believe it? TRY IT! What do you have to LOSE?

If you find yourself carrying on any negative conversation, break it, even though it might give you pleasure, as it does for many other people; they too might find the same fun in being critical. Breakaway, especially from the negative inner conversation, which we all easily fall victim to.

So, today if you are not happy with the world in which you live, blame no one, but turn within to these gifts and use them wisely, for here we are told to order our life according to our conversations. And you can change it only by changing the conversation because the conversation is equated with who you are.

> *"To be successful in real estate, you must always and consistently put your clients' best interests first. When you do, your personal needs will be realized beyond your greatest expectations."*
>
> ~ Anthony Hitt

> *"I think if people are passionate about something, it could be real estate or biochemistry, and that spark gets turned on in them, everyone's beautiful in that zone."*
>
> ~ Cindy Crawford

When I entered my real estate career in 2002, I thought my previous success already achieved that, my financial future in real estate was a done deal. How naïve was my thinking! It would be many years later before I would discover the settling winds of knowledge to guide me on a conquest to find the truth. It is said that the thoughts you think, that you will become.

Over the years, there have been those real estate experts and gurus who have brought forth their opinions and thoughts on the subject. With endless debate as to why so many new real estate agents do not make it in the profession, very little, I believe, has been spent on positive mental development. Industrywide, if there was more implementation of the mind science to it with more focus spent touching on growing the mental side of possibilities to one's business with spending less on the archaic physical way of building one's real estate career.

These shifts or changes to what now could develop in making the difference in elevating one to a true understanding of success. And the best part; the one learning the concepts would have a complete understanding that it's the mental side that powers the physical side of their business with truly unlimited potential.

> **It is said that the thoughts you think, that you will become.**

> **If you think you are a failure, so you become.**

> **If you think you are a success, a success you will be.**

Let's face it; no one intentionally desires to fail in life, but fear of failure is what destinies our demise when the seeds of thoughts are lacking. If you think you are a success, a success you will be. Let's face it; these ideas and practices are not taught in any formal school, nor are they learned in the workplace.

Many people are trained and educated to be just a little bit smarter than the equipment they operate without very little focus to expand someone's potential beyond. FEAR is the #1 largest obstacle preventing someone from realizing his or her true untapped potential, and it's all within one's mind.

For one to experience the mind science to this, one should have a clear understanding of the operant power of the mind and, importantly, realize the journey of revelation goes beyond this five senses world we all live in. What moves the world we see before our very eyes are 99% mental and 1% physical. If you don't quite understand? Let me elaborate. Everything that you see in this material world of sight, sound, taste, smell, and touch was brought into existence by thought. The very chair you sit on, to the table you may dine on, to the car you may drive, were each once a creation in someone's mind, their imagination. The imaginational act of that person's creation now converted through thought into a tangible item or service whereby being observed by our five senses is the very embodiment of the creative power of thinking.

How does this relate to real estate and your career? All creation of thought begins within the mind! Good, bad, or indifferent thoughts will manifest through this five senses world as a result. What prevents us from realizing our full potential is the fear-based thinking or programming we allow into our imagination. Fear has MORE destructive power than a demolition crew of 1,000. Until one learns to harness the raw power of a positive mind, a person will continually be subject to and be the slave to his or her own negative thoughts and poor inner conversations. One must learn to achieve the right concentration and willpower, for when harnessed together can enable us to materialize thoughts for the intended desires of our life.

> *"Arm yourself with the knowledge and understanding of mind, and all other things will automatically happen for one's good."*

If one is to understand the steps to success, we must understand why so many fall short of it by comprehending the mechanics behind this puzzle, and find why this is easily overlooked. For one to receive more understanding must study closer the imaginal acts of one's mind. When you go into your imagination, make sure that you are actually performing the action, hearing the words, touching the object, or smelling the aroma in your self-conceived drama. What you do in your imagination is not merely daydreaming, in which you see events in your mind's eye. You must enter the dream *(imagination)* as if you were actually there. You must make "then" now and make "there" here. To make this perfectly clear, imagine that you would experience driving a new car after you have achieved your goal. In that case, you would not merely see a new car in your mind's eye. You must actually enter the dream. Feel yourself seated behind the steering wheel. Smell the newness of the interior. Feel yourself enjoying a comfortable ride. Feel the happiness that would be yours after accomplishing your dream. When seeing your new career in your mind, you must make "then" now and make "there" here to create; you must self-conceive the real estate drama of success with the imaginary acts and rolls you desire to see with inner positive thoughts.

One must learn how to hold every thought captive to begin to quantify the impact on one's self, for good or bad. It doesn't matter what you have been taught; you can change your beliefs, and by doing so, change the circumstances of your life.

Conscious and Subconscious terms Differentiated

You must remember that these are not two minds. They are merely two spheres of activity within one mind. Your conscious mind is the reasoning mind. It is that phase of mind, which chooses. For example, you choose your books, your home, and your partner in life. You make all your decisions with your conscious mind. On the other hand, without any conscious choice on your part, your heart is kept functioning automatically, and the process of digestion, circulation, and breathing are carried on by your subconscious mind through processes independent of your conscious control.

Your subconscious mind accepts what is impressed upon it or what you consciously believe. It does not reason things out like your conscious mind, and it does not argue with you controversially. Your subconscious mind is like the soil, which accepts any kind of seed, good or bad. Your thoughts are active and might be likened unto seeds. Negative, destructive thoughts continue to work negatively in your subconscious mind, and in due time will come forth into an outer experience that corresponds with them.

The conscious mind is sometimes referred to as your objective mind because it deals with outward objects. The objective mind takes cognizance of the objective world. Its media of observation are your five physical senses. Your objective mind is your guide and director in your contact with your environment. You gain knowledge through your five senses. Your objective mind learns through observation, experience, and education. As previously pointed out, the greatest function of the objective mind is that of reasoning.

Remember, your subconscious mind does not engage in proving whether your thoughts are good or bad, true or false, but it responds according to the nature of your thoughts or suggestions. For example, if you consciously assume something as true, even though it may be false, your subconscious mind will accept it as true and proceed to bring about results, which must necessarily follow, because you consciously assumed it to be true.

Power of the Subconscious Mind

The power of your subconscious is enormous. The subconscious mind never sleeps, always working 24/7 even when you're asleep. Whatever thoughts, beliefs, options, theories, or dogmas you write, engrave or impress on your subconscious mind, you shall experience them as the objective manifestation of circumstances, conditions, and events in your life.

Your subconscious mind cannot argue controversially. Hence, if you give it wrong suggestions, it will accept them as true and will proceed to bring them to pass as conditions, experiences, and events. All things that have happened to you are based on thoughts impressed on your subconscious mind through belief. If you have conveyed erroneous concepts to your subconscious mind, the sure method of overcoming them is by the repetition of constructive, harmonious thoughts frequently repeated, which your subconscious mind accepts, thus forming new and healthy habits of thought and life, for your subconscious mind is the seat of habit.

The habitual thinking of your conscious mind establishes deep grooves in your subconscious mind. This is very favorable for you if your habitual thoughts are peaceful and constructive. Be careful, any negatively subjected to the subconscious and impressed with feeling and emotion, will, in a short order of time, accept it as true. Begin to realize that your conscious mind is the "watchman at the gate," and its chief function is to protect your subconscious mind from false impressions. You are now aware of one of the basic laws of mind: Your subconscious mind is amenable to suggestion. As you know, your subconscious mind does not make comparisons or contrasts; neither does it reason and think things out for itself.

If your desire in life is not to fail, then stop defining one's self by the words that demonstrate failure. Begin to define yourself by the words of prosperous, successful, and wealthy. When saying, "I am not successful," that is your self-definition expressed. That is your self-awareness—and when thought you are never going to be able to experience anything better than, or anything other than, your self-definition.

Your subconscious also plays an important part in your financial life. Have you ever come across people who always had money no matter what?

Some may have been frugal people, but I'm sure you've seen those who were rich but were also big spenders. And then you've seen those who always worked hard but were still broke. Then there are people who hardly ever work and always have money.

What's going on here?

The truth is it has to do with their subconscious...their inner financial thermostat is set on a certain level.

How can you set your thermostat higher to attract more?

The answer may surprise you. It is hard for most people to attract wealth because they have the wrong attitude about money. Some religions teach people that there is something noble in being poor and struggling. Sayings like "Money is the root of all evil" makes people have negative feelings towards money. At first, you may say, "I don't believe any of these," but again, these may be deep-seated unconscious triggers that you may not be aware of.

Experiments conducted by Merle Lawrence (Princeton) and Adelbert Ames (Dartmouth) in a psychology laboratory at Hanover, N.H., prove that what you see when you look at something depends not so much on what is there as on the assumption you make when you look. Since what we believe to be the "real" physical world is actually only an "assumptive" world, it is not surprising that these experiments prove that what appears to be solid reality is actually the result of "expectations" or "assumptions." Your assumptions determine not only what you see but also what you do, for they govern all your conscious and subconscious movements towards the fulfillment of themselves.

Therefore, as you approach your new career in real estate, in essence, if you see yourself a success, a success you will be. On the other hand, if you see yourself a failure, a failure you will be. The decision is all yours, which "assumption" you can see, regardless of whether it's real or not.

> *"Respect your efforts, respect yourself. Self-respect leads to self-discipline. When you have both firmly under your belt, that's real power."*
>
> ~ Clint Eastwood

> *"Success is not the key to happiness. Happiness is the key to success. If you love what you are doing, you will be successful."*
>
> ~ Albert Schweitzer

There is a GREAT cliché I've heard, and when asked by others who have triumphed, many will say it has worked great for them, it's "Fake it till you Make it." No, I am not saying one must go out to a new career and become some imposter or fraud. No! Quite the contrary. All reason and logic may deny the facts of a person's current state of consciousness or reality, but if one believes with all faith, it will harden into fact in this physical world we all see.

Reprogramming Your Subconscious Mind

Your subconscious mind has immense power in controlling your life experiences: from the types of food, you eat to the actions you take each day, the level of income you earn, and even how you react to stressful situations. Every bit of it is guided by your subconscious beliefs and interpretations.

In short, your subconscious mind is like the autopilot feature on an airplane. It has been pre-programmed to follow a specific route and you cannot deviate from that route unless you change the directions programmed into it first.

What Is The Subconscious Mind?

The "subconscious" is the part of your mind that operates below your normal level of waking consciousness.

Right now, you're primarily using your conscious mind to read these words and absorb their meaning, but beneath that mental focus, your subconscious mind is busily working behind the scenes, absorbing or rejecting information based on an existing perception you have of the world around you.

This existing perception began forming when you were an infant. With every experience, your subconscious mind soaks in information like a sponge.

It rejected nothing while you were young because you didn't have any pre-existing beliefs to contradict what it perceived. It simply accepted that all of the information you received during your early childhood was true.

You can probably see why this becomes a problem later in life! Every time someone called you stupid, worthless, slow, lazy, or worse, your subconscious mind just stored the information away for reference.

You may also have received messages about your potential in life or limitations you'll face based on your physical abilities, skin color, gender, or economic status.

By the time you were 7 or 8 years old, you already had a solid foundation of belief based on all that programming from people in your life, television shows you watched, and other environmental influences.

How Does this 'Did' Programming Affect You Now?

Now that you're an adult, you may think that you can simply discard the hurtful or untrue messages you absorbed during your early life, but it's not quite that simple.

Remember that all of this information is stored below your level of conscious awareness. The only time you become aware of it is when it limits your progress in creating a balanced, successful, and productive life.

Have you ever tried to achieve a goal and kept sabotaging yourself at every turn? Maddening, isn't it? It's important to know that you're not defective or doomed to fail, no matter what you do.

More likely, you've got some old programmed messages that conflict with the new conditions you want to create.

This is excellent news because it means you can achieve just about anything if you first take the time to reprogram your subconscious mind!

The Programming Is Still Going On

Before we discover how to reprogram your subconscious, it's important to know that the programming still continues to this day. With every experience you have, you draw certain conclusions and store the messages that will guide your future actions.

For example, what kind of message do you think would be stored if you were rejected by someone you cared about?

Your subconscious mind (that clever detective) would immediately go hunting through your memories and find other examples of rejection (like that time your best friend dumped you to hang out with the more popular kids) and draw a conclusion that you're somehow unworthy or unlovable and deserve to be rejected.

Now, here's the interesting thing: if you have an experience that conflicts with an already established belief, your subconscious mind will either reject it or reframe it, so it goes along with your existing view of reality.

Here's an example: Let's say you have an underlying belief that you're unattractive, and an attractive person expresses an interest in getting to know you better.

Most likely, the first thing you're going to think is that it must be a joke or a cruel trick. You won't believe that this person could find you attractive because you already believe that you're unattractive.

Beneath the surface of your conscious awareness, your subconscious mind is screaming, "No way!! This person is way too attractive to be interested in me; something isn't right here..."

Then you'll either reject that person before they can reject you, or otherwise do something to sabotage what could have been a great relationship.

The same thing happens when you struggle to achieve your goals. Eventually, you start to believe that you aren't capable of success, so you come to expect failure and end up doing just that over and over again!

You can probably imagine many other situations where your subconscious mind limits you, but reprogramming it is a simple matter if you know-how.

- First and foremost, believe in yourself.
- Understand what is holding you back so you can overcome it.
- Spend time in quiet self-reflection, prayer, or meditation at least once a day.
- Guard everything that enters and leaves your mind.
- Know what you want in very specific terms.
- Remove all sources of negativity from your life.

- Surround yourself with success-minded people.
- Create a realistic plan to attain your deepest desires.
- Take positive steps each day toward what you want to attract.
- Focus on the present - as if you've already attracted the things you want.
- Create visual reminders of your goals.
- Make a recording of your favorite affirmations or buy a self-hypnosis CD.
- Avoid conflicting messages by matching your feelings with your desires.
- Write a newspaper report about your success as if it has already happened.
- Be an advocate for yourself.
- Have an attitude of gratitude.
- Choose to carry a positive attitude at all times.

Impress the Subconscious

Once you have decided what is sought in the level of achievement for your career, it's essential that you continually impress your subconscious mind with the idea of having it. Two of the best ways to impress the subconscious mind are affirmations and two just before falling into the drowsy state of sleep; visualize your desires to be achieved before drifting off to sleep.

An example may be to begin impressing your subconscious mind with a vision of meeting a potential home seller arriving at their property. Experience seeing yourself in your mind, walking through the home telling the seller, yes, indeed, your home will sell. Can you smell the aura of the house, and feel the sight of seeing the company real estate sign with your name on it placed in the seller's yard and the joy it makes feeling and knowing that it's DONE, the home is SOLD. Remember, your subconscious will bring to pass any picture held in the mind backed with faith.

- Define yourself as the one who is DOING that which you want to do.

- Define yourself as the one who is HAVING that which you want to have.
- Then visualize. See yourself in your own mind being, doing, and having the good, which you desire.

Conscious and Subconscious Mind

A great way to be acquainted with the two functions of your mind. Look upon your own mind as a garden. You are a gardener, and you are planting seeds "thoughts" in your subconscious mind all day long, based on your habitual thinking. As you sow in your subconscious mind, so shall you reap in your body and the world around.

Subconscious thoughts are different from conscious ones in that they have a self-developing nature that is predisposed towards keeping our body, particularly our involuntary bodily functions, in optimal condition. The subconscious mind's self-development nature is available to you every second of every day, not only when you are slumbering, and it is always looking for areas or issues where it can prevent damage or provide assistance to your body. The subconscious is always in harmony with limitless motivations, inspirations, and ideas that are easily accessible for you to tap into and use for your own purposes.

The subconscious mind does not only receive messages, but also communicates with us through our presentiments, intuitions, hunches, feelings, and instincts. It is forever showing us the way to achieve advancement, growth, and transcendence in order for us to realize greater successes. Humans are also known for their helpfulness towards others in need, which is, in turn, a reflection of our subconscious in action. One example of this subconscious influence on us all happened way back in 1906, after the Great San Francisco Earthquake.

After the great disaster struck, a multitude of disabled, crippled, and bedridden patients left their hospital beds and came to the rescue, executing unbelievable acts of valor and bravery. Despite the danger surrounding them and their physical handicaps, their subconscious mind's influence came through, compelling them to save lives, even though they themselves were at a disadvantage.

Such is the power of the subconscious and its well-meaning instinct to help, turning the crippled into heroes in the process, by ultimately making them take such courageous steps they couldn't have accomplished without its assistance.

Highly renowned and world-class authors, composers, singers, and artists also tap onto the vast and unlimited powers of the subconscious mind to provide them the inspiration to create, innovate, and change the world with their groundbreaking works and ideas committed to paper, canvas, or song. Inspiration and ideas do come from within, and that wellspring of motivation and encouragement - the so-called muses of Ancient Greek Mythology - is nothing more than subconscious influence at work.

Begin now to sow thoughts of peace, happiness, right action, goodwill, and prosperity. Think quietly and with interest on these qualities and accept them entirely in your conscious reasoning mind. Continue to plant these beautiful seeds "thoughts" in the garden of your mind, and you will reap a glorious harvest. Your subconscious mind may be likened to the soil, which will grow all kinds of seeds, good or bad. Every thought is, therefore, a cause, and every condition is an effect. For this reason, you must take charge of your thoughts to bring forth only desirable conditions.

When your mind thinks correctly, when you understand the truth, when the thoughts deposited in your subconscious mind are constructive. Harmonious and peaceful, the magic working power of your subconscious will respond and bring about smooth conditions, agreeable surroundings, and the best of everything. When you begin to control your thought processes, you can apply the powers of your subconscious to any problem or difficulty. In other words, you will be consciously cooperating with the infinite power and omnipotent law, which governs all things.

Look around you wherever you live, and you will notice that the vast majority of humanity lives in the world without, and the more enlightened men are intensely interested in the world within. Remember, it is the world within, namely your thoughts, feelings, and imagery that makes your world without. It is, therefore, the only creative power, and everything that you find in your world of expression has been created by you in the inner world of your mind, consciously or unconsciously.

Thoughts and Ideas to Remember

1. Arm yourself with the knowledge and understanding of mind, and all other things will automatically happen for one's good.
2. FEAR is the #1 largest obstacle preventing someone from realizing his or her true

untapped potential, and it's all within one's mind.

3. Become definite about what you want from your real estate career --- and you will know how to get it – by using your power of visualization!

4. Everyone in the world is seeking happiness – and there is one sure way to find it. That is by controlling your thoughts. Happiness doesn't depend on outward conditions. It depends on inner conditions.

5. Every thought is a cause, and every condition is an effect.

6. A person must practice separating oneself from the negative moods and thoughts during all the troubles and disasters of daily life.

7. If you can imagine it and you visualize it, you can create it.

8. Change your thoughts, and you change your destiny.

Recognition of this truth will transform you from one who tries to make it so, into one who recognizes it to be so.

Chapter 3

Whatever You Add To, "I Am"

Whenever I say, "I AM," I AM [is] creating something. Now, you can lie and not believe what you are saying, but you cannot think something about "I am" and not create it. We are creating morning, noon, and night by our "I am" statements. If you say, "I don't feel well," and you believe it, you are perpetuating illness in your life. You must change those statements to "I feel great."

It is a great disservice to people to teach them this kind of negative self-image psychology. Because whatever you define yourself as, whatever you say about yourself, that is what you become. And the only way that you are going to become something else, or become what you want to be is to re-define yourself as that which you want to become. When adding or saying anything after the words of "I AM" that you will become! One must watch every thought that contains I Am. If you are observant, you will see that you have created every circumstance and experience of your life.

If you believe that, "I AM" successful, then you MUST be. If you believe that "I AM" a real estate magnate home listing machine, then you MUST be. If you think you are, you WILL be. So, begin to monitor every word (I AM) that you say. Do you see a pattern? Don't the circumstances of your life reflect what you have been saying? You have been misusing the creative power of (I AM). Now that you are aware of what you have been doing, watch every word and make it conform to what you wish to bring into your life and real estate career.

Don't be tied down to the conditions that one may find themselves in. Don't be locked in and bound by the undesirable circumstances that one may find themselves in. Change the details by changing one's self-image by changing the self-definition of SELF.

A person can decree a thing, and it will come to pass. If today, a person is ordering that which is appearing in that person's world, and he or she shall continue to do so as long as the person is conscious of being self. In saying it another way, it is being aware that your thoughts do affect your real estate career.

Nothing has ever appeared in this world, but what a man or woman decreed that it should. This you may deny, but try as you will, you cannot disprove it for this decreeing is based upon a changeless principle. A man or woman does not command things to appear by their words, which are, more often than not, a confession of his or her doubts and fears. Decreeing is ever done in consciousness.

It is more important to go through the motions and activities of the world of real estate within your conscious mind, then the physical act itself. The physical actions will always follow all the mental decrees of the mind.

The Power of Words

Words have POWER! Our very word can bless our real estate business, or they can curse our every endeavor by the very thoughts we choose to believe.

Every person will automatically express that which he or she is conscious of being. Without effort or the use of words, at every moment, humanity is commanding oneself to be and to possess that which one is "conscious" of being and possessing.

Having discovered, through an uncritical observation of the reactions to life, a self that must be changed, one must now formulate a desire. That is, you must define the one you would like to be instead of the one you indeed are in secret. With this desire clearly defined, one must, throughout the conscious waking day, notice one's every reaction regarding this desire. The reason for this is that everyone lives in a certain state of consciousness. Whereby which states of consciousness we have already described as the total of his or her reactions to life. Therefore, in defining a desire, you are defining a state of consciousness, which, like all states of consciousness, must have its reactions to life. For example: if a rumor or an idle remark could cause an anxious reaction in one person and no reaction in another, this is definite proof that the two people are living in two different states of consciousness.

Disempowering Words

The majority of us have been given many negative suggestions. Not knowing how to thwart them, we unconsciously accepted them.

Here are some of the negative suggestions:

"You can't," "You'll never amount to anything," "You mustn't," "You'll fail," "It's not what you know, but who you know," "the world is going to the dogs," "You haven't got a chance," "It's no use trying so hard," "You're all wrong," "It's no use," "What's the use, nobody cares," "You're too old now," "Love is for the birds," "Things are getting worse and worse," "Life is an endless grind," "You just can't win," "Watch out, you'll get a disease," "You can't trust a soul," etc.

A person's failure to get results may also arise from such statements as, "Things are getting worse." "I will never get an answer." "I see no way out." "It's hopeless." "I don't know what to do." "I'm all mixed up." When a person uses such words or statements, they get no response or cooperation from there subconscious mind. They will be lost only to their own negative thoughts and beliefs and wonder why the world doesn't move them; that person will get nowhere.

Whatever You Can See, You Can Be

If you want something in the profession of real estate, then see yourself with it. See yourself being, doing, and having the good you desire. See what you want and feel yourself experiencing it. Your positive thinking and feeling will lead you to make the right decisive action to accomplish the wishes of your desire.

A person's process of thinking forms the impressions in that person's mind; these impressions, in turn, become manifested as facts and experiences in his or her life. A builder visualizes the type of building he wants; he sees it, as he desires it to be completed. His imagery and thought processes become a plastic mold from which the building will emerge - a beautiful or an ugly one, a skyscraper, or a very low one. His mental imagery is projected in his mind and is drawn on paper. Eventually, the contractor and his workers gather the essential materials, and the building progresses until it stands finished, conforming perfectly to the mental patterns of the architect.

Consciously claim yourself to be that which you seek; appropriate the consciousness of that which you see into your daily reality. The importance of objectively observing one's thoughts cannot be stressed enough. It is easy to slip into thought patterns that can hinder us in achieving our desires. It then becomes easy to blame others or attribute our frustrations to the second cause. Begin to observe your thoughts; do not be discouraged if you find that your inner conversations do not match the way you would feel if you have achieved your goal. You must first become aware of what you are doing with your creative power before you can begin to change it.

If one desires to reach for success in real estate, then one needs to become conscious of being that success visually. And continue to be aware of being in that state of success until that which you are conscious of being is perfectly expressed. A person only needs to say with feeling in their heart, "Yes, I shall believe, and it shall come to pass."

Habitual thought is indicative of character. The way to change the outer world in one's life is to make the inner conversations and actions match the outer conversations and actions of the fulfilled desire. It is believing to make the, "Unseen Seen" by fulfilled desire. All reason and logic may deny the facts of a person's current state of consciousness, but one believes with all faith it will harden into fact in this physical world as reality.

The reason for lack of faith on the part of one is that a person may look at the desired state through the consciousness of his or her present limitations. Therefore, one naturally sees it as impossible of accomplishment. One of the first things a person must realize is that it is impossible, in dealing with this mental law of consciousness, to put new wine into old bottles or new patches on old garments. That is, one cannot take any part of the present consciousness into the new state. For the state sought is complete in itself and needs no patching. Every level of consciousness automatically expresses itself.

The mental law is simply reflecting and giving back to you exactly what you are focusing on with your thoughts.

Whatever is appearing in your world now, although it seems real and an unalterable fact, it is a reflection of previous activity in your consciousness. Therefore, a change in consciousness will reflect that change in the future just as surely as past beliefs reflect the present. A person is pure formless consciousness, and that which one conceives himself or herself to be is an illusion or reflection of the particular ideas that a person holds true.

These illusions exist only so long as a person focuses his or her attention upon them and gives them life. The conscious mind forms beliefs and opinions from the evidence of the senses or the perceived outer world. The creative power within each of us accepts as true that which the conscious mind impresses upon it. Your creative power takes those ideas, which are thought of with feeling, and projects them in your outer world. It is important to remember that not all thoughts are creative. Only those which are believed to be true or which are joined with feeling create the circumstances and events that you will encounter.

To rise to the level of any state of consciousness is to become that state in expression automatically. But, to increase to the degree that a person is not now expressing, one must altogether drop the consciousness with which a person is now identified. Until a person's present consciousness is lost or released, one will not be able to rise to another level. A mental picture is worth a thousand words.

Your imagination is the power to save you from whatever circumstances you now find yourself. You can experience your heart's desire through the use of your imagination. Nothing is impossible for your imagination. Your imagination is unlimited in what it can accomplish. If you can imagine something, you can achieve it. Let me give you an example. If you were unable to walk and were confined to a wheelchair, you could close your eyes and imagine yourself running on the beach or wading in the water. If you would imagine yourself doing this until it took on the vividness of reality, you could accomplish healing that would allow you to walk or run.

The way to use your imagination creatively is this. Relax in a chair or on a bed and close your eyes. First, determine what it is you wish to experience. Then, in this state of complete relaxation, bring to mind the final result of what it is you desire. In other words, if you were seeking a promotion at work, the final result might be that people would congratulate you on your promotion. You might move to a larger office. You would enjoy an increase in pay. Take any one of these events and, with your eyes closed, actually hear your friends congratulate you on your promotion. Feel their hand in yours as they tell you how happy they are for you. By actually feeling that you are being congratulated, your imagination will go to work to bring about that state in your outer world.

You need not be concerned about how this will be accomplished. Your imagination will use whatever natural means are necessary to bring it about. "I am the beginning and the end." "My ways are past finding out." What you do in imagination is an instantaneous creative act. However, in this three-dimensional world, events appear in a time sequence. Therefore, it may take a short interval of time to realize in the outer world what you have just experienced in imagination. After you have performed this act in your imagination, open your eyes and go about your regular, natural affairs, confident that what you have done must come to fruition in your world. Make your inner conversations conform to your imaginal act. You have planted a seed, and you will soon see the harvest of that which you have sowed. Your positive thinking and feeling will lead you to make the right decisive action to accomplish the wishes of your desire and take your real estate career to a higher level of achievement.

Programming Your Subconscious for Wealth

The state of your finances, believe it or not, has a lot to do with the state of your mind. If your subconscious believes that you are poor, then it is more than likely that you will face endless financial problems. Unless you change your state of mind, you will have trouble making ends meet. Remember that thought is power, and your subconscious has the power to manifest all that you believe.

The most common problem that people have is the belief that wealth and fortune can only come from tireless hard work. It is more than likely that you were raised with ideals that strongly suggest the idea that in order for you to be rich, you have to toil and suffer through hard work, and that nothing comes easy.

Even though you may have heard about ingenious entrepreneurs who have freed themselves from the "rat race" and are making a ton of money working just a few hours a day, you might think that you could never accomplish such a feat. So it shouldn't be a surprise when you find yourself having to struggle to get by financially.

This idea of how the only road to wealth has to be a long, laborious, painstaking one has been so deeply ingrained into the subconscious that it becomes near impossible to change the way you think about your own fortune. You would be surprised to know that there are many paths to wealth, and they are not necessarily inaccessible to the common man.

I have a friend in Texas who earns a six-figure salary. He makes it a point to go on frequent trips around the world via cruises or first-class flights. He truly believes that he is a person of high net worth, and deserves every bit of his six-figure salary. He admits that there may be employees in his company who probably know more about the business than he does, but he is also of the mind that they earn one-tenth of what he earns because that is what they believe they are worth. They have never taken steps to improve their finances in any way, and they lack the creative drive and ambition necessary to change their fortune.

The important thing to keep in mind is that the concept of wealth is an idea, a belief, a seedling that is subject to the laws of manifestation. It is your belief that will set your subconscious mind to work in bringing into reality your idea of what wealth should be. Through subtle conscious awareness, your mind manifests the kind of wealth that you have envisioned for yourself.

If you believe that you are meant to not have the kind of wealth that you have envied others for having, you will never attain such wealth. Fill your thoughts with poverty and hardship, and so shall your life be filled with poverty and hardship.

Remember that your subconscious lacks the ability to reason and rationalize; it merely takes your conscious mind's direction and records the necessary information. Persisting with beliefs of financial inadequacy will only result in despair.

But when you force your subconscious to believe in the idea that you are a person of high financial worth and abundance, you will gain access to a treasure trove of inspiration and intuition that will aid you in your desire to attain your ideal wealth.

If you think you are a success, a success you will be.

CHAPTER 4

NEW CAREER STATISTICS

New real estate agents do not always have excellent guidance early on. People who elect to work as solo agents from the start, for instance, are typically left to figure out what works on their own.

Real estate, in general, has a significant turnover every few years, and the newer agent is usually the majority of that equation. At times, it might be mentioned at various real estate training seminars, and one might see a real estate article, but rarely does anyone speak about the specifics of the "why" when it comes to new agent turnover.

What are some of the causes?

Companywide real estate brokers are reluctant to talk about the high turnovers of new agents entering the business in part when the new agent joins that office they may find the educational resources or training in that office spread too thin from the start. An agent may overcome some of those education hurdles or lack thereof with the right positive thoughts and creative imagination needed, and jump to a real estate office with the right approaches for his or her career.

One might think, wouldn't it be better if the real estate broker had a better plan to help the new agent to triumph and do well. Maybe if by emphasizing the positive brainpower side of thinking and include many of the sales techniques to real estate, instead of continually dealing with the fallout from losing those agents. One might try to capitalize more on the understanding of the conscious side of positive thinking. Don't get me wrong! Many of these larger companies and real estate franchises have unique training programs to assist in developing a new agent's skills and develop the agent's sales techniques, which could rival the most experienced agent in the business. But none of this matters until one understands the significance of the Mind Science and power responsible for what moves everything.

Sales Technique

Due to my early years of an unconscious misunderstanding of the "Burning Desire" for success, I was unaware of the most critical mechanics behind it. I could not identify those qualities for nearly a decade. As a man think it, so is he. One must assume a person has a reasonable understanding of the mind power within oneself so that when adding to the new agent the needed training programs and superior sales techniques, the complete embodiment of knowledge and success can NOW take root.

When looking at the statistics in real estate, it is precisely that, a record of who will make it and who will not but takes no part into the account of what happened. Unless someone analyzes the data and researches what is behind the failure rate, then it's pretty useless. But, for all intense purposes, one may figure for every ten real estate agents entering the business within six months, half of them will be gone due to lack of *(poor planning)* money and *(lack of vision)* frustration. As the year comes to an end, maybe 1 or 2 agents from the first ten might achieve traces of success. From the achievement of those couple of agents surpassing the others, one could justify the feelings of early success with an income to match for the reward of accomplishment.

A large percentage of new agents leave the industry after just a few short years as a result.

First-year earnings for most new agents with little to no experience entering the industry can be from $0 to $25,000 annually. Furthermore, for every 100 new agents entering the industry, maybe 8 or 9 of the 100 agents will make close to or at a 100k net commission for their 1st year.

If you think you are a success, a success you will be. This is the vision and mental mindset one must possess if one is to pursue a career in real estate or for anything if that matters.

Today we are in the wealthiest environment, in history, of technology for real estate. For the younger generation, they may call this the Internet Social Marketing Age for real estate. I have found it to be important to have some working knowledge and a fundamental understanding of marketing. Having some intermediate skills with both, whether it's hands-on or monitoring from a close distance, will save you time and money. For the inexperienced internet user or real estate agent, many internet marketing companies will find you without you trying. Many of these companies range website development to AdWords with google for website rankings. Other companies might have their own specialized - video or audio - services, maybe a deployment of a business Facebook or Instagram page to providing content for your LinkedIn page.

Most internet marketing companies are reputable, but some of these companies may use questionable sales techniques to boost your ego by using words like, "some so-and-so TOP agent referred them to you because you're a top name in the area," or "in the industry, your name had been coming up quite a bit lately." Be cautious when approached by companies with this type of sales tactic. If an internet marketing company must stroke your ego or use scripted words to work, your mind's ego, be careful. It may cost you BIG in the end. Personally, my knowledge was more than ample with both the internet and marketing; I had enough skill to design my own website. Use your own intuition when forming a plan to market yourself and your services, faith, and belief will never misguide your direction.

Money and Resources

Once a new agent realizes the cost associated, with getting a real estate license, it doesn't take very much in spending close to $2,500 or more for some real estate classes, cram preparation classes, state testing, state licensing, fingerprinting, MLS dues, Keycard dues, and REALTOR® Board dues, and you're all about set. RIGHT?

BUT WAIT!

There is more. Don't forget the monthly office dues, the cost for business cards, For Sale signs, and Open House signs and much more before you have a seat at your new real estate office. Also, let's not forget that it is recommended that you have a financial cushion of at least 6 to 9 months to keep you sustained while embarking on your new career.

If you are like most people when it comes to finances when entering this career, within the 1st month or two, you're just about tapped out funds with all the costs involved in starting your real estate career. It was for me! Having the thought of spending an additional $500 to $1,500 a month, marketing oneself was almost unimaginable.

I almost became a statistic in my first year, but my unconscious misunderstanding of "Burning Desire" for success is what continued with driving me further. I was unaware of the most critical mechanics behind my success in real estate, the thoughts of my Mind.

> *"All power is from within and therefore under our control."*
>
> ~ Robert Collier

Of the people I have had the opportunity of training and mentoring, some have become wildly successful even more so than myself. It always brings great excitement to hear their story and what impact I might have in assisting the advancement of their knowledge and expanding their direction of success in real estate.

In many instances, when a person is seeking a career in real estate, they need that concise direction when applying the mind power of positivity and real estate technical sales approach to building one's career; with enough time, everything will fall into place.

Numbers in any business are vital. A real estate business is no different. Many factors determine success, but one essential aspect is the vision needed and imagination required to see success when the objective world around you denies the very reality of it.

The numbers within a real estate office from the higher-ups are seldom spoken about unless it's the office broker or manager working to grow their agent population. Not to say there is anything wrong with that, but to the new real estate agent interviewing various real estate offices, one needs to find the right fit and not cave into just the company name. While some real estate offices have a keen sense of not only growing their office, they also put resources into retaining their top agents. Other real estate offices put a considerable amount of resources into new agent development and training specifically. As a new real estate agent, one must have a plan in effect for that type of real estate office suited to that person's personality and focus on what will work best for you.

When searching where to hang your real estate license, there is no right or wrong real estate office to work for. The agent who is deciding on a real estate office will need to find clarity with any internal office prospect policies and training programs available. One ultimate question in every new agent's mind should be, what is being taught relevant, and if applied, can it help me in my new career? Selecting the right real estate office can make or break a new agent who ultimately is seeking a pathway to success.

See yourself in your own conscious mind being, doing, and having the good, which you desire. At this moment, try to notice your inner state of thinking. To what thoughts are you consenting? With what feelings are you identified? You must be ever careful where you are within yourself.

Winston Churchill departed this world a very successful man; however, during his life, he had many failures. Then one day, he made this discovery, which changed his life. These are his words: "The mood decides the fortunes of people, rather than the fortunes decide the mood."

Those who compare their thoughts and feelings to the inside instead of what appears on the outside; win the game of life. And the game is lost by those who do not recognize this mental law. Being consumed by anger, they see no change in their world. But if they would change their mood, their circumstances would change. Then they would recognize the law behind their world.

See yourself in your own conscious mind being, doing, and having the good, which you desire.

Chapter 5

Naysayers and No

Naysayers are people who tell you that you can't do anything right in their eyes. In the world of real estate, you will find plenty. They're not offering constructive criticism or helping you prepare for the challenge ahead, and they're people who give you every reason under the sun why things won't work out.

Sometimes it's not even what they say – it's the expression on their face or the way they throw doubt on your plans by looking at you like you've lost the storyline to destiny.

They think they're helpful, but they're harmful to be around if you want to follow your dreams. I think these people are subconsciously jealous and worried that if you end up succeeding, it'll only highlight their failure to follow their dreams.

Whether they're aware of it or not, they're trying to drown your ambition. They're happy to have a life half lived, and they want to keep you where you are. If you listen to the naysayers, you will never achieve your dreams. Importantly, see yourself in your own conscious mind being, doing, and having the good, which you desire.

One doesn't have to look too far; naysayers are everywhere. They're often 'well-meaning' members of your own family who protest they're only showing concern by advising caution or people you consider good friends who 'only want the best for you.' But there's a BIG difference between motivating and supporting someone and trying to stop them from achieving their full potential.

Positivity Yourself

So, surround yourself with positive, motivated, supportive people and don't tell the naysayers your plans. Just do your own thing, follow your dreams, make your own life, forge your way, and show them what success can genuinely look like.

> *"Tune out the naysayers, tune into your own courage, and take a bold step toward the passion-filled life you really want."*
>
> ~ Oprah Winfrey

> *"If I would have listened to the naysayers, I would still be in the Austrian Alps yodeling."*
>
> ~ Arnold Schwarzenegger

You cannot help your real estate career by focusing on negative things as you focus on your negative events, you not only add to them, but you also bring more things that are negative into your own career. You have the ability to tap into the unlimited supply of mental power through your thoughts and feeling and bring those into your experience.

When you focus your thoughts on something within your real estate career and you maintain that focus, you are in that moment commanding what you want with the highest power of the mind, your imagination. Your thoughts will become things, and your career in real estate will never be the same once you grasp the power of the mind.

Understanding not just what you do professionally, but also why you chose to do it in the first place. It's an enlightening thought that helps real estate companies and individuals understand the values and motivations that lead them to do what they do. When you take your focus away from the what of the moment, (your pitch being rejected by a prospective customer,) and turn it to the why, (you want to provide for your family, buy a house, pay off loans, etc.,) it automatically puts the rejection into perspective.

Win with Rejection

Now instead of having a short-term view of the rejection as an impossible dead-end, you see it for what it is: a speed bump on the road to success. You know why gives you the motivation to power through success, to stay focused, and to prove to yourself and others that a momentary setback doesn't keep you from aiming after your more significant purpose.

To take advantage of the success secrets of handling a "no," it's important to remember something crucial: When a customer says no, they aren't saying no to you.

The home may be a bad fit for the customer; it may be the wrong area. And even if the rejection feels personal (and hey, some of them do,) it could be something as simple as you caught the prospect on a bad day. Or maybe they had some bad experience with a real estate agent in the past. Regardless, if you take the rejection personally, you're missing a massive opportunity for a win.

You can still win through a rejection. Your prospect may not choose to buy, but you may still be able to help them with a problem or educate them on an issue. You can walk away from a rejection leaving a positive view of yourself and your company with the prospect. And that can lay the foundation for a future win because rejection isn't forever.

Sometimes the NO's can really get us in places we unconsciously cannot see it. I once knew a real estate agent I was friends within our office. One day in discussing some matters with him and I discovered after speaking with him that two months previously, he had become more irritated, annoyed, and resentful toward a particular home seller who, after some time had promised to sign a listing contract, and had withdrawn at the last moment. He began to live in the unconscious fear that other future clients would do the same, thereby setting up a history of inner frustration, fear, and disbelief. He gradually built up in his mind a belief in obstruction and last minute cancellations until a vicious circle had been established. He exclaimed, "What I fear most has come upon me." My friend realized that the trouble to his real estate business was in his own mind and that it was essential for him to change his mental attitude.

Great Success Affirmations

One MUST remember when adding or saying anything after the words of "I AM" that you will become! Become aware and begin to monitor every word (I AM) that you say.

If you believe that, "I AM" successful, then you MUST be. If you believe that "I AM" a real estate magnate home listing machine, then you MUST be. If you think you are, you WILL be.

- I AM a money magnet. I always attract abundance and prosperity easily and effortlessly into my reality.
- I AM successful; success follows me everywhere I go.

- I always spot opportunities and utilize them. New doors are always opening for me.
- I AM attracting success and prosperity with all of my great ideas.
- The possibilities and opportunities in my life are endless.
- I AM successful in all that I do.
- I AM thankful for the opportunities that come my way.
- I give generously, and I receive generously.
- I easily attract sales.
- I AM free of negative thinking. I embrace only positive thoughts and ideas.
- Wealth comes to me easily and effortlessly.
- I AM in charge of my emotions, desires, and abilities.
- Success is my natural state, and I AM grateful for all the universe gives to me.
- I AM a perfect match for my real estate business ideals.

- I AM inspired, enthusiastic, and success bound.

Robert Frost once said, "Our founding fathers did not believe in the future; they believed the future in." The most creative power in you is your power to believe a thing in. Our founding fathers did not believe that the passage of time would produce this country as they desired it. They wanted democracy, not a monarchy, and knew that sitting down and hoping it would come to pass wouldn't do it - they had to appropriate it, so they simply believed it in. How? By faith. They subjectively appropriated their desire.

Words have POWER!

ABOUT THE AUTHOR

When my real estate career began in 2002, I, like so many others, approached it with all the excitement and passion, a can-do attitude. Within eight months, I was all but out of a real estate career until one day when a profound game-changing experience would be revealed, and my real estate career would instantly transform.

Before entering real estate, I was in another profession as I acquired my real estate license in mid-2002. In my prior field of work, I had the honor to be among the top in the insurance industry and thought immediately upon entering the real estate profession I made the naïve assumption I would be an instant SUCCESS. Keep in mind; I was not aware of the actual mechanics of success, let alone in a position to speak about success. At the time, it was an unknown illusion for me. All that was going for me in my favor was an unconscious misunderstanding of the "Burning Desire" to succeed.

Most real estate offices say they are the best in training real estate agents; mine was no different. I was taught how to master writing contracts and listing agreements, how to prospect, send out postcards, prepare mailings, and many more things. With the sense that my real estate trainers were true wizards of real estate knowledge, I was sure to hit it BIG.

Seven months went by after attempting many failed prospecting methods to generate home sales, also while taking into consideration the guidance of my office broker, coaching from various real estate trainers, and words of wisdom from other experienced agents. I HAD NOTHING! Not seeing the BIGGER picture, I still had no direction at what appeared to be a not so promising future in real estate. Now entering the eighth month, I began to discover how wrong those expectations were, I found myself saying, "That was ok, things will change," but they didn't.

As my frustration mounted, the 10th month was nearing with no real sun on the horizon for my real estate career, and stress was settling in. My inner soul searching took over. My thoughts began to ponder, "I may need to seek another career...", (see a negative thought) like so many find themselves thinking when things are not working out in business. Nevertheless, I kept telling myself, "I'm a fighter; I will find a way." This was one of my darker moments in life. All I was living on now was, "Hope and Faith," I had nothing else left.

Not too long after, I had a friend who was making it wildly successful in real estate. Still financially stumbling in my career to find my niche, I approached him with reluctance; I contacted him by phone, hoping for that magic pill of success. When I spoke with him, I told him my little short story of how I was, "desperately searching," to find a way to make it in real estate.

Later in that week, I met up with him at an *Open House* he was hosting in Del Mar, California. His name was Kevin, and what he would say to me that day would set me on a path to change my thinking about my real estate career. What Kevin did that day that I unconsciously failed to see, and it wouldn't be until 15 years later that I could see. It had nothing to do with my selling techniques or his skill at training, but it had everything to do with my conscious mind seeing the vision and believing with feeling in my heart the "magic pill" was the way to success.

When saying I attempted everything back in 2002, that would be an understatement. Even as late as writing the book: *Art of the Open House*™, in 2018,

I still was no closer to understanding the much-needed revelation behind it all.

The most essential component that I had failed to see during this time was the Mind Power needed to make the difference. Without understanding the power of the subconscious mind, all attempts to grasp hold of success will fade into the sunset. A person's destiny cannot be seen if the mind is stuck in the past, learn from the past, live in the present, and create a new future.

The thoughts you think, are the thoughts you become.

If you think you are a success, a success you will be.

RJ Salerno

BOOKS AVAILABLE

- *Art of the Open House*™
- *Real Estate Success Secrets*
- *El Arte de la Casa Abierta*™ (Spanish Edition)
- *L'arte della Casa Aperta*™ (Italian Edition)
- *Eyes of a Real Estate Professional*
- *Mobile Home Tycoon*

www.ingramcontent.com/pod-product-compliance
Lightning Source LLC
Chambersburg PA
CBHW020450220526
45464CB00002B/936